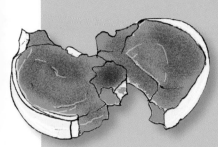

Healthy Eating

Meat Fish and Eggs

Susan Martineau
and Hel James

W

FRANKLIN WATTS
LONDON • SYDNEY

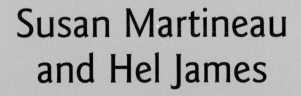

An Appleseed Editions book

First published in 2006 by
Franklin Watts
338 Euston Road
London NW1 3BH

Franklin Watts Australia
Hachette Children's Books
Level 17/207 Kent Street
Sydney NSW 2000

Created by Appleseed Editions Ltd,
Well House, Friars Hill, Guestling, East Sussex TN35 4ET

Designed and illustrated by Helen James
Edited by Jinny Johnson

ISBN-10: 0-7496-6720-6 3-3
ISBN-13: 978-0-7496-6720-7
Dewey Classification: 641.3' 06

A CIP catalogue for this book is available from the British Library

Photographs: 9 Mark Peterson/Corbis; 10-11 Ed Lallo/Zuma/Corbis; 13 Bohemian Nomad
Picturemakers/Corbis; 15 Robert Dowling/Corbis; 16 Owen Franken/Corbis; 17 DiMaggio/Kalish/Corbis;
18 Tim Thompson/Corbis; 21 Macduff Everton/Corbis; 22-23 Jeffrey L Rotman/Corbis; 24-25 Paul A
Souders/Corbis; 27 PhotoCuisine/Corbis; 29 David Reed/Corbis.
Front cover: Envision/Corbis

Printed and bound in Thailand

Contents

Food for health   4

A balanced plateful!   6

Body-building foods   8

A beefy treat   10

Sheep and lamb   12

Pigs and pork   14

Meat for keeps   16

Meat with a difference   18

All about chicken   20

Food from the sea   22

Oily fish   24

Fish in a shell   26

Excellent eggs   28

Words to remember   30

Index and websites   32

Food for health

Our bodies are like amazing machines.
Just like machines, we need the right
sort of fuel to give us energy and
to keep us working properly.

If we don't eat the kind of food
we need to keep us healthy we
may become ill or feel tired and
grumpy. Our bodies don't really
like it if we eat too much of one
sort of food, like cakes or chips.

We need a balanced diet.
That means eating different
sorts of good food in the
right amounts.

You'll be surprised at how much
there is to know about where our
food comes from and why some
kinds of food are better for us
than others. Finding out about
food is great fun and very tasty!

I'm hungry.
I wonder what's
for dinner.

Chicken, fish and eggs all contain lots of protein.

Let's go and find out.

Protein foods help to keep us healthy.

A balanced plateful!

The good things or nutrients our bodies need come from different kinds of food. Let's have a look at what your plate should have on it. It all looks delicious.

Rice, bread and pasta

These foods contain carbohydrates and they give us energy. They are also called starchy foods. About a third of our food should come from this group.

Fruit and vegetables

Rice, bread and pasta

Chicken with rice and vegetables is a great balanced plateful.

6

Fruit and vegetables

These are full of great vitamins and minerals and fibre. They do all kinds of useful jobs in your body to help keep you healthy. About a third of our food should come from this group.

Milk, yogurt and cheese

These dairy foods give us protein and also calcium to make strong bones and teeth.

Meat, fish and eggs

Protein from these helps your body grow and repair itself. They are body-building foods and you need to eat some of them every day.

Sugar and fats

We only need small amounts of these. Too much can be bad for our teeth and make us fat.

Milk, yogurt and cheese

Sugar and fats

Meat, fish and eggs

Water

We need to drink at least 6 glasses of water every day.

Body-building foods

We need body-building or protein foods so that we can grow muscles, bone, hair and skin. Protein also repairs our bodies if we are ill or we hurt ourselves.

Who eats fish? Who eats meat?

I've got lentil and vegetable stew.

Meat, fish and eggs are fantastic protein foods. If you don't want to eat meat, you can get protein from dairy foods, nuts, pulses (like lentils and beans) and from tofu, which is made from soya beans. People who don't eat meat are called vegetarians.

Butchers and restaurants buy meat from a meat market like this one.

Who is a vegetarian?

I've got a lamb chop and vegetables.

I've got cod with tomato sauce.

You don't have to eat steak three times a day to get all the protein you need. If you are eating a balanced plateful your body will be getting plenty of body-building goodness.

A beefy treat

Beef is the meat we get from cows. Cows kept for their meat are called beef cattle and there are cattle farms all over the world. When the animals are big enough to be used for meat they are taken in special trucks to a market to be sold.

Steaks, like sirloin and rump, come from the back of the animal.

Meat from the legs and front is good for stews.

Beef is full of protein, iron, zinc and B vitamins. Iron keeps our blood healthy and zinc helps us fight off illness. B vitamins help our bodies turn our food into energy.

Fat check

Beef is quite a fatty meat so we should not eat too much of it. Look out for pieces of meat that are labelled lean as this means they have less fat in them.

You don't need to eat a lot of beef. Small amounts of meat with some vegetables in a stir-fry make a great balanced meal.

Hearty stews include pieces of meat and lots of healthy vegetables too.

Sheep and lamb

Lamb is the meat that comes from sheep.
Sheep are also kept for their wool and milk.
A mother sheep can have up to three lambs a year.
When the lambs are old enough, the farmer takes
them to market to be sold for meat.

Sheep live in large groups called flocks. In some countries, like Australia and New Zealand, there are thousands of sheep living on giant farms called sheep stations.

Lamb gives us the same goodness or nutrients as beef and is very tasty. But we should not eat it too often as it also has quite a lot of fat in it.

Add vegetables such as onions, peppers and tomatoes to pieces of lamb to make kebabs — a delicious balanced meal.

You can buy leg of lamb as well as shoulder of lamb and lamb chops.

Roast lamb is lovely, but it's best to trim off the fat!

Pigs and pork

Pork is the meat we get from pigs. Some pig farmers keep their pigs outside. The pigs only go indoors to sleep or have their babies. Other farmers keep their pigs in big buildings and they don't go out at all. Some people think that the pork from the outside or free-range pigs tastes better.

Streaky bacon

Pork fillet

Pork is full of protein and other nutrients but some pork, like pork chops, is very fatty. Pork is also made into sausages, ham and bacon and these also contain a lot of fat. Pork fillet, or tenderloin, is quite lean and is the healthiest way to eat pork.

Slices of ham

Pork chops

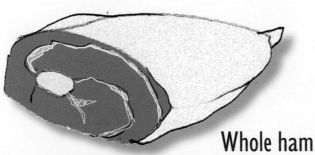

Whole ham

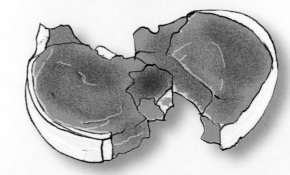

A mother pig can give birth to two litters of piglets a year, with as many as 12 in each litter. The piglets drink their mother's milk and they grow very fast. They are sold for meat when they are about six months old.

Meat for keeps

Before fridges were invented it was difficult to keep meat fresh. People had to think of ways to stop it going bad. They used to cure or keep meat by putting it into salty water, or they rubbed it with salt, then dried it. Sometimes the meat was smoked over a fire.

This piece of pork is being rubbed with salt to preserve it.

Salted and smoked meats taste nice and so meat is still processed in this way today. The trouble is that these meats are not very good for us. They have lots of salt, fat and other chemicals in them. They are best eaten just every now and then.

Ham
There are many different kinds of ham. See how many you can find when you go to the shops.

Bacon
Bacon is sold in slices called rashers. The bacon is salted and sometimes smoked too.

Can you count how many hams are hanging from the ceiling in this shop?

Salami
Salami is made from pork and sometimes beef.

Meat with a difference

Other animals are also kept for their meat. It might seem quite strange to eat creatures such as ostriches, deer and buffalo, but their meat is very good for us. This meat has lots of protein, vitamins and minerals but less fat than beef, lamb and pork.

The biggest bird in the world

The ostrich is certainly bigger than a chicken, but its meat is just as tasty.

Herds of deer

The meat we get from deer is called venison.

Buffalo beef

These animals are kept not only for their meat but for their milk too.

Liver

Lambs' kidneys

We can also get meat from the inside parts of animals. This is called offal. The liver, heart and kidneys of animals are very good for us as they contain lots of vitamins.

Pieces of kidney are used in steak and kidney pie.

19

All about chicken

Chickens are farmed all over the world for their eggs and their meat. Chicken farms that keep the birds for their meat are called broiler farms. Chickens and other birds which are farmed for us to eat, such as turkeys, geese and ducks, are often called poultry.

Which one of these delicious dishes would you choose?

Chicken meat is very good for us. It gives our bodies protein but has less fat in it than beef, lamb and pork. It does not contain quite as much iron or zinc but has lots of B vitamins to keep us healthy.

Tandoori chicken

Chicken soup

On some broiler farms the chickens live inside huge buildings and are given special food to make them grow quickly. On free-range broiler farms the chickens can go outside during the day and scratch for their own food. They come indoors at night to be safe from foxes!

Roast chicken

Chicken salad baguette

Food from the sea

Fish is a great way to eat protein. It also gives our bodies vitamins and minerals. There are so many types of delicious fish to choose from. Try to eat fish about twice a week if you can.

White fish

Cod, haddock, plaice, sole, turbot and halibut are all white fish. Their flesh (or meat) has hardly any fat in it. White fish can be cooked in different ways. Grilled, baked or steamed fish is best for us. Deep-frying fish in oil is not so healthy.

Freshly frozen

Fish should be eaten up very quickly after it has been caught. Freezing it is a way of keeping it for longer. A lot of fish is frozen on factory ships as soon as it is caught.

Fillets of fish are good to eat.

They are tasty and there are no bones!

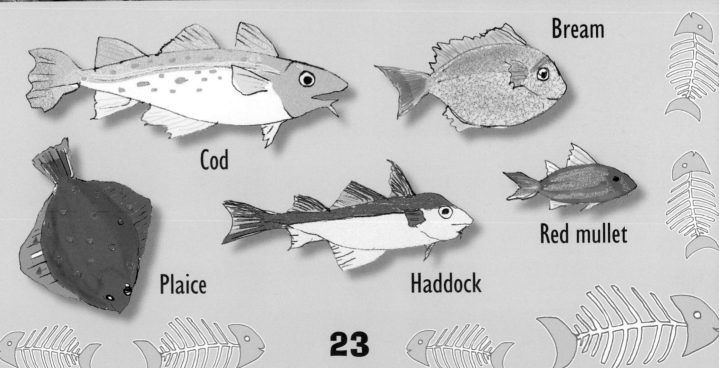

Bream

Cod

Plaice

Haddock

Red mullet

Oily fish

Salmon, trout, herrings and sardines are all oily fish.
Oily fish is very good for you as it contains loads
of the vitamins A and D as well as protein.
The oil in the fish also helps to keep you healthy.

Fish on a farm?

Fishing boats catch most of the fish we eat but
some, like salmon, can be farmed. The fish live
in large floating cages and are fed special food
to help them grow. Some people think that
these farms are not good for the environment.

Sardine

Mackerel

Anchovy

Sea trout

Salmon

Fish in a tin

Oily fish, such as salmon and sardines, can be put into cans and keeps very well for a long time. Have a look in your store cupboard and see what kinds of canned fish you have.

Fish in a shell

Shellfish are not really fish, but different kinds of sea creatures. All have a tough shell to protect their body. There are many kinds of shellfish such as mussels, crabs and prawns. See how many you and your friends can think of. How many have you tried eating?

Prawns

Shellfish is full of protein and vitamins, but it must be eaten when it is very fresh. It is often frozen before being sent to the shops so it can be kept for longer.

Clams

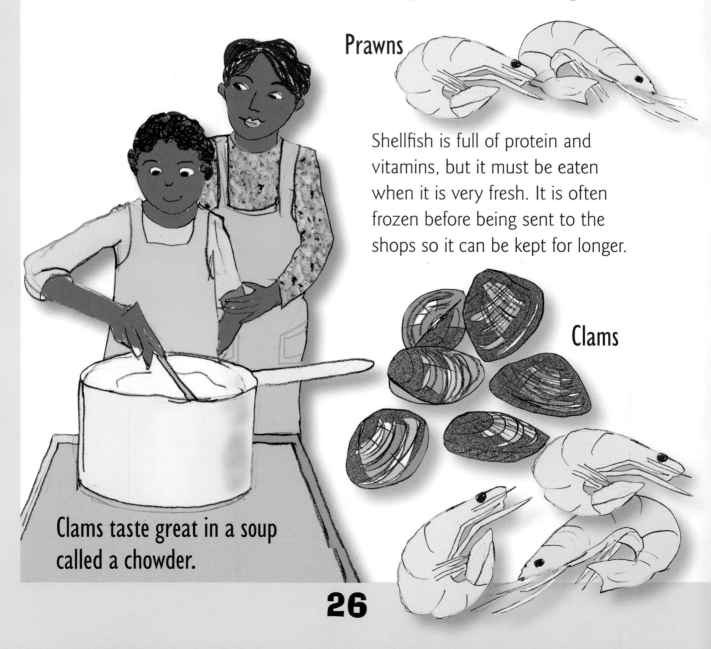

Clams taste great in a soup called a chowder.

You can eat oysters fresh from the shell.

Mussels and prawns are used to make a delicious Spanish dish called paella.

Oysters

Prawns

Mussels

Lobster

Crab

Crabs and lobsters are cooked and then served in their shells.

Excellent eggs

A chicken lays an egg nearly every day. Egg farmers keep chickens specially to lay eggs for us to eat. The eggs we eat are not fertilized and do not have chicks inside them.

Look what's in an egg!

Iron for your blood

Vitamin A for your eyes

Zinc to fight off illness

Body-building protein

B vitamins to keep your body working properly

Vitamin D and calcium for making strong bones and teeth

Power pack

All eggs are checked and sorted into sizes before being packed into boxes for the shops. An egg is full of goodness for our bodies.

Thousands of battery chickens are kept together in a rows of very small cages. Many people prefer to buy eggs that come from free-range hens.

Some egg farms are free-range. The chickens can wander about outside and find food. They lay their eggs inside a hen house where they sleep at night. Other farms keep thousands of chickens inside giant buildings in rows of small cages. These are called battery farms. The eggs from these chickens roll down on to a conveyor belt.

Egg quiz
Ask your friends how they like to eat eggs and find out the most popular dish. Do they prefer them poached, scrambled or made into omelettes?

Words to remember

broiler farms   Chicken farms where the birds are kept for their meat.

calcium   A mineral that helps build healthy bones and teeth.

carbohydrates   Starches and sugars in food that give us energy. Carbohydrate foods are rice, pasta, bread and potatoes.

conveyor belt   The moving part of a machine that carries things from one part of a farm or factory to another.

cured   To salt, smoke or dry meat or fish so that it will keep for longer.

dairy foods   Foods made from milk, such as cheese, butter, cream and yogurt.

environment   The world around us.

factory ships   Fishing boats that catch large amounts of fish, clean it and freeze it too.

fertilized   When an egg is fertilized a chick will grow inside it.

fibre   This is found in plant foods like grains and vegetables. It helps our insides to work properly.

flock   A large group of animals.

free range   Free-range animals are allowed to live and roam outdoors.

iron   A mineral in food that we need to keep our blood healthy.

lean   Meat without fat on it.

minerals   Nutrients in food that help our bodies work properly. Calcium, iron and zinc are minerals.

nutrients   Parts of food that your body needs for energy, to grow healthily and to repair itself.

offal   Meat from the insides of animals, like the kidneys, liver and heart.

processed   Many foods are processed which means they go through some changes before they reach your plate. Some foods are more processed than others. Frozen food has been processed, so have cured and smoked meats.

protein   Body-building food that makes our bodies grow well and stay healthy.

rashers   Slices of bacon are called rashers.

sheep stations   The huge sheep farms of New Zealand and Australia.

venison   The meat from deer.

vitamins   Nutrients in food that help our bodies work properly. Vitamin A is good for our eyes. There are several B vitamins. They help turn our food into energy and keep our muscles, skin and blood healthy. Vitamin D helps our bodies to use calcium to make strong bones and teeth.

zinc   This mineral helps our body fight off illness and repair itself when we hurt ourselves.

Index

bacon 14, 17
battery farms 29
beef 10-11
broiler farms 20-21, 30
buffalo 18-19

chicken 6, 20-21
cows 10

deer 18-19

eggs 20, 28-29

fish 22-23, 24-25

ham 14, 17

lamb 12-13

meat 9, 16-17

offal 19
oily fish 24-25
ostriches 18-19

pigs 14-15
pork 14-15
protein foods 5, 7, 8

salami 17
salted and smoked meat 16-17
sheep 12-13
shellfish 26-27

vegetarians 8-9
venison 19

WEBSITES

General food information for all ages
www.bbc.co.uk/health/healthy_living/nutrition

Food Standards Agency – healthy eating, food labelling
www.eatwell.gov.uk

Quizzes and games on food
www.coolfoodplanet.org

Information and games on healthy eating
www.lifebytes.gov.uk/eating/eat_menu.html

Worksheets and activities
www.foodforum.org.uk

Practical advice on healthy eating
www.fitness.org.uk